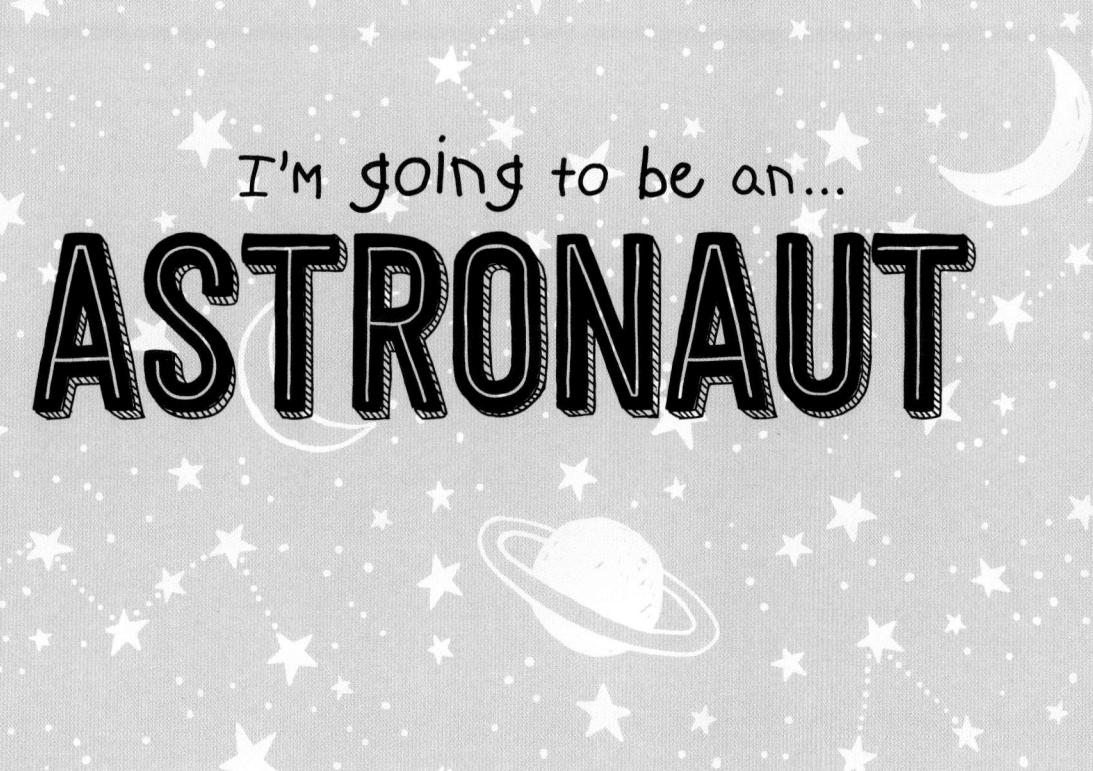

AUTUMN
PUBLISHING

Written by Suzanne Fossey
Illustrated by Junissa Bianda

Designed by Richard Sykes
Edited by Suzanne Fossey

Copyright © 2020 Igloo Books Ltd

Published in 2021
First published in the UK by Autumn Publishing
An imprint of Igloo Books Ltd
Cottage Farm, NN6 0BJ, UK
Owned by Bonnier Books
Sveavägen 56, Stockholm, Sweden

All rights reserved, including the right of reproduction
in whole or in part in any form.

Manufactured in China. 0721 001
10 9 8 7 6 5 4 3 2 1

Library of Congress Cataloging-in-Publication
Data is available upon request.

ISBN 978-1-80022-861-0
autumnpublishing.co.uk
bonnierbooks.co.uk

I'm going to be an...
ASTRONAUT

AUTUMN PUBLISHING

I will fly all the way into space, and travel to planets no one has ever seen.

I'll need lots of different tools to get my spaceship ready.

I'll learn how to use every single one.

I'll have my own space suit. It will have a round helmet, chunky boots, and gloves that make my fingers look like sausages.

This is it! It's time to go.

5... 4... 3... 2... 1...

BLAST OFF!

In space, I'll sleep standing up and use special equipment to exercise every day so that I stay strong.

I will eat my food before it floats away. And I'll wear disposable clothes, because you don't have to do laundry in space!

I'll jump in my space rover and ZOOM around the craters like a racing driver.

I'll have to be really good at math and science so I can do experiments.

I'll do what no one else has ever done and fly to the very **EDGE OF SPACE.**

People will say that's impossible...
but I'm still going to try!
Maybe I'll pop out the other side.

When I grow up, I'll do all these things.

But I've got lots of other things to do first.

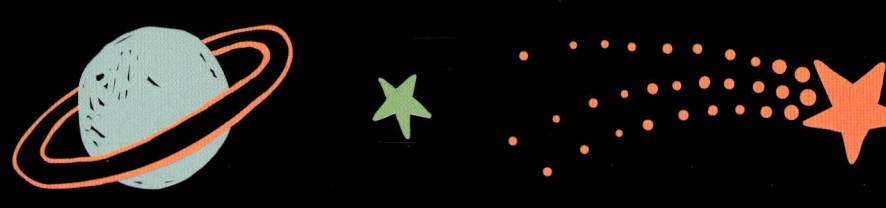

BEING AN ASTRONAUT

Astronauts fly up away from the Earth into space. They are scientists and explorers, finding out more about our planet and the universe beyond.

Astronauts have to be good at science and math. They also have to be healthy and strong, as getting into space is hard work, like riding a super-fast rollercoaster.

Astronauts have traveled to the Moon, and soon they might be able to visit Mars. Exciting new missions are being planned all the time. Who knows where you could go?

Matteo Cabrera
302